crazy for JC!

It's all here! Learn about your favorite 'N Sync guy, JC Chasez!

How did JC get his start on *MMC*?
Where did he get the nickname "Big Daddy"?
How does he deal with his success?
Could *you* be the perfect girl for him?

Find all these answers and more in . . .

'N Sync with JC!

'N SYNC
with
JC

Nancy Krulik

AN ARCHWAY PAPERBACK
Published by POCKET BOOKS
New York London Toronto Sydney Tokyo Singapore

AN ARCHWAY PAPERBACK *Original*

An Archway Paperback published by
POCKET BOOKS, a division of Simon & Schuster Inc.
1230 Avenue of the Americas, New York, NY 10020

ISBN: 0-671-03277-1

First Archway Paperback printing March 1999

10 9 8 7 6 5 4 3 2 1

AN ARCHWAY PAPERBACK and colophon are registered trademarks of Simon & Schuster Inc.

Cover photos courtesy of London Features International

Printed in the U.S.A.

IL 4+

For two budding musicians, Amanda and Ian. We'll see your names in lights someday!

contents

'N SYNC
with
jc

does this sound
like you?!

- Do you scream whenever you hear JC's voice broadcasting through the radio and into your room?

- Do you give JC's pic a big kiss every morning when you wake up, and another smooch at night before you go to bed?

- Have you named your new guinea pig (dog, cat, gerbil, fish, bird, llama) JC?

- Have you ever written, e-mailed, or called magazine editors, asking them to put more posters of JC in their issues?

- Do you sign your first name with last name Chasez—just to see how it would look?

- Have you written Santa asking him to leave JC under your tree?

- Do you spend hours practicing fifty different ways to start up a conversation with JC—just in case you ever meet?

- Have you already read this book ten times, and used your highlighter to underline the most important info?

If you answered yes to any of these questions, you are definitely crazy for JC! But don't worry, you're not alone! The dark-haired, blue-eyed lead singer of the hot pop group 'N Sync is a favorite with girls all over the world!

It's hard to believe that it has only been a

year since 'N Sync released the American version of their platinum selling self-titled debut album. But ever since then, the guys have been tearin' up the hearts of girls all over the country—playing to sold-out crowds, appearing on TV shows, accumulating platinum and gold records, and even managing to have two albums (*'N Sync* and *Home for Christmas*) on the *Billboard* Top Ten at the same time.

The five guys in this pop music phenomenon—JustiN Timberlake, ChriS Kirkpatrick, JoeY Fatone, Lance "LansteN" Bass, and JC Chasez (= 'N SYNC. Get it?) are all unbelievably talented musicians and dancers. And they are all drop-dead gorgeous. But lately it appears that one guy is standing out in the crowd. And that guy is JC.

It's tough to put your finger on what it is about JC that makes girls' hearts skip a beat. It's not just that he's the one with the fanciest footwork. (Have you ever seen his flips?) It's not even the fact that he sings lead on some of the group's most romantic songs. (Wouldn't you go "Sailing" with him any time?) It's more that JC has a quiet charisma which can't be explained, but is definitely there.

Let's face it. Once you've looked into JC's hypnotizing blue eyes, there's no turning back. You're 'N Sync with him forever! His fans all agree on one thing: JC, God Must Have Spent a Little More Time with You!

When you're crazy about someone, you want to know everything about him—from the very moment he was born until the present hour. You want to know what makes him happy, what makes him sad, what makes him scared, and especially what makes him fall in love. You want to know what his future holds, and when and where you might meet up with him (or at least catch him on a TV special).

Well, as 'N Sync might say, "You Got It."

You'll find everything you ever wanted to know about JC Chasez right in this book. So don't waste another minute. Turn the page and get reading!

1
the arrival of the shy guy

On August 8, 1976, in Washington, D.C., Karen and Roy Chasez welcomed a new baby boy into the world. They named him Joshua Scott Chasez. (FYI: you pronounce JC's last name Sha-se; the z is silent.)

As a baby, young Josh (as his parents called him) seemed cute and adorable. But there were certainly very few signs that he would someday grow up to a be a star of mega proportions, singing to crowds of thousands of screaming fans.

In fact, the opposite was true. As a little kid, JC was very shy. Although he would sing and dance in front of the mirror in the privacy of his own room (his parents say they knew he had musical talent by the time he was age three), it wasn't his style to put on shows for family and neighbors.

JC and his parents moved to Bowie, Maryland, a suburb of Washington, shortly before JC's younger sister Heather was born in 1979. Two years later, Heather and JC welcomed baby Tyler to the Chasez family.

JC and his sibs are totally the products of a typical suburban childhood. They went to a local elementary school, played sports with their neighborhood friends, and went on family vacations—sometimes driving for weeks in their car, seeing how many states they could visit. (Before joining 'N Sync, JC's total was thirty-eight states. His career has now taken him to almost all fifty!)

JC is very appreciative of the warm family life he experienced as a child. He knows how lucky he is to have parents who love and support their kids, and who want to spend time with them. (It couldn't have been easy for Karen and Roy to go driving around the country with three little screaming Chasezes in the backseat!)

Some people really rebel against a suburban upbringing. They make it their business to dis the malls, the car pools, the basement boy-girl parties, and the school dances that define life in American suburbia. But JC has never been down on his upbringing. In fact, he and the rest of the guys in 'N Sync celebrate the suburban culture.

"Our image is really ourselves," he explains. "You know [in their music] gang bangers preach about the lives in the streets, and they are heroes to some people. We're kids from suburbia, and we're singing about having a good time, because we want to have a good time and we want everyone around us to have a good time!"

Knowing how privileged he was while he was growing up has made JC especially sensitive to the plights of people who don't have a nice home to grow up in. He feels a great responsibility to help those who are less fortunate than he is. So, when his incredibly busy schedule allows, JC takes the time to volunteer at homeless shelters, making lunches or serving meals to the families who are there. It's just his way of giving something back to society.

Like many suburban kids, JC had a stereo in his room. So did his siblings. And there were clock radios, car stereos, and portable tape players around, too. In fact, music was everywhere in the Chasez home. Music played an *especially* huge part in the family's holiday celebrations. At Christmastime his family would travel to JC's mother's parents' house and sing Christmas carols. Later the family would sing songs as they opened their gifts.

Although neither of JC's parents were musicians, Karen and Roy always made sure to let their children know that they valued music as an art form, and as a valid career choice—something not all families do.

Karen and Roy felt it was important to expose their children to all forms of music, including pop, classical, and jazz. JC took a special liking to jazz music, which remains his favorite to this day .

That early musical exposure has stayed with JC all his life. "When music was introduced to me for the first time, I fell in love immediately," JC wrote in the liner notes for the 'N *Sync* CD. "Thanks to a great many people, my love for it grows stronger every day."

But music wasn't JC's *whole* life when he was a kid. Even back then, JC always had an eye for the ladies. (And who could refuse JC's blue eyes!) He was only six years old and in the first grade when he got his very first kiss. The lucky girl's name was Lea Thompson. (JC's Lea is no relation to the actress who plays Caroline on *Caroline in the City* today.)

By age eleven, he'd gone on his first date. "It was at a party," JC recalls. "I met this girl and we danced together. I didn't leave her side the whole night."

Although he was not a bad student, JC did have trouble being behind a desk all day at school. Sitting still has never exactly been JC's big strength. During those seemingly endless hours in the classroom, he was the kid whose feet were tap-tap-tapping restlessly under the desk. Luckily, it was during his elementary school years that JC discovered sports.

Sports were the perfect outlet for the energetic young JC. He had always been extremely physically agile, and he always enjoyed being around a lot of friends. Football in particular was a great release for JC's restlessness, and playing on a team fulfilled his need for male camaraderie. (Not surprisingly, JC says he enjoys being part of 'N Sync for exactly the same reasons!)

JC has never abandoned his love of football. In fact, when he feels like unwinding, he likes to toss around the pigskin with his group mates. But even football couldn't replace JC's love of music and dance.

When he was a preteen, JC's nimble footwork and striking good looks made him a standout at school dances. Eventually some of his friends asked him to dance with them at some local talent competitions. He managed to bring home first-place trophies from several of those competitions.

Eventually, JC's overwhelming success as a dancer gave him the confidence boost he needed to finally sing in front of an audience—albeit as part of a group. It would be several years more before he felt comfortable enough to take on a solo.

One day in 1990, while JC's mother was reading the local paper, she came upon an ad announcing auditions for *The Mickey Mouse Club* TV show *(MMC)*. Although she wasn't sure if JC was confident enough to audition for the show, she was certain that he had the talent to go all the way. So, she casually mentioned the advertisement to JC and some of his friends.

But it wasn't JC who originally took his mother's hint. It was a friend of his who first decided to audition for the show. JC only agreed to go to the auditions with his pal to provide moral support.

Deep in his heart, JC figured that going on the audition would pretty much be a waste of his time. After all, it was his first professional audition, and JC knew that performers don't usually score the first gig they try out for.

But JC went anyway and waited in line with about five hundred other hopefuls from the Washington area. (Nationwide, more than twenty thousand kids auditioned for the show.)

What happened next was the kind of story old-time Hollywood movies were made of. Rather than choosing JC's buddy, the *MMC* producers made a beeline straight for JC.

"They picked me out of a large crowd and asked if I could wait," JC recalls. "Finally, after about ten hours, the casting director came and told me that he thought I would be perfect for the show."

Only twelve kids from the Washington audition made it to the next stage—a callback which included a screen test. In the end, JC wowed everyone involved with casting *MMC*, and became one of the new Mouseketeers.

Before he knew what was happening, JC was signed to a contract for the 1991 *MMC* season, and he and his dad were on their way to Florida for six months to tape episodes of *MMC*.

We guess you could say that everything else that has happened to JC professionally is part talent, part hard work, and part Disney magic!

2
who's the leader of the club . . . ?

It should come as no surprise that JC got his start on *The Mickey Mouse Club* children's show. Talented teens have been setting off skyrocketing careers from the *MMC* launch-pad for almost fifty years!

The Mickey Mouse Club was one of the very first children's television shows. It was broadcast in glorious black and white back in 1953. The show was based on an idea that Walt Disney himself had. Walt wanted to create a show filled with kids who weren't typical showbiz kids.

"Don't get me those kids with tightly curled hairdos that tap dance. Get me children who look like they're having fun. Then later we can teach them to tap dance or sing, or whatever," Walt reportedly told his TV producers.

So the producers went around the country and hung out in school yards, looking for ordinary kids with not-so-ordinary charisma.

In the end they gathered a group of kids, taught them to sing and dance, and created a major hit for early television. The show's format was simple—a little singing, a little dancing, and some skits and continuing serials (which were kind of like mini–soap operas), all starring the Mouseketeers.

The first Mouseketeer to become an international star was Annette Funicello. In the 1950s, Annette was America's dream teen. She made movies and recorded pop tunes that sold in the millions. She got much more fan mail than all the other Mouseketeers combined. She was so popular that the Disney people canceled the show completely when Annette became too old to be a Mouseketeer, even though the ratings were still high.

Since Annette Funicello, there have been plenty more Mouseketeers who have gone on to big careers, including Ryan Gosling (hunky star of *Young Hercules*), Keri Russell (better known as TV's *Felicity*), Lisa Whelchel (you'll find her as Blair on old *The Facts of Life* reruns), and singing stars Christina Aguilera and Britney Spears.

In the early 1980s, the Walt Disney Company brought back *The Mickey Mouse Club* on their new cable channel, the Disney Channel. At first the show was called *The New Mickey Mouse Club*, but that was soon changed to the hipper, cooler *MMC*.

MMC pretty much followed the same format as the original *Mickey Mouse Club*. It was just a bunch of normal kids, singing, dancing, acting, and having fun. It's just that the kids' clothes were much funkier and their songs a lot hipper than they were on the old show. Oh, and the kids didn't have to wear those mouse ears with their names written on them.

Like the original show, *MMC* was broadcast after most kids were home from school, making sure it got the largest audience possible. The show had a very loyal following, and the kids at home really got to know the teens who starred on *MMC*, even though at any one time there were twenty teenagers in the cast and the cast kept changing. As people grew up, or moved on in the hopes of starting singing or acting careers, they were replaced with fresh faces. JC was part of the cast for the last four seasons of the show.

MMC proved to be the ultimate training ground for JC. For one thing, it got rid of his shyness once and for all. Although it wasn't until his third season on the show that JC got his guts up to sing a solo, he did learn to sing harmonies on camera with the other cast members, and as backup for guest stars on the show. JC also got a chance to act, taking on the part of Clarence "Wipeout" Adams on the *MMC*'s serialized drama, *Emerald Cove*.

The Mouseketeers often got to perform with popular singers and entertainers. Working with famous people taught JC a valuable lesson—how to stay humble when the world is turning you into a hero. "It is incredible to meet famous performers who are just the nicest people in the world and are so down to earth," JC told a Florida reporter in 1992.

After the show's fifth season, JC and several other cast members (including Keri Russell) had the opportunity to go into the recording studio to work on the *MMC* soundtrack (it's out of print, but sometimes you can find it on Internet swap or sale sites), and learn about how the recording industry works. The Mouseketeers also toured around quite a bit, singing the national anthem at Mighty Ducks hockey games, and performing at the Disney-MGM Studios for visitors to the park. The live performances gave JC experience singing in front of large screaming crowds. (Bet that comes in handy these days!)

While he was living in Florida, JC spent a great deal of his off-set time improving his dancing. He spent hours working with a gymnastics trainer trying to perfect his flips—a skill that is still much appreciated today by his 'N Sync fans. This extra practice came in handy since his high energy level made him a favorite of the *MMC* choreographers, and he was often given some of the show's tougher footwork to perform. JC also worked with a vocal coach to learn how to control his perfectly pitched pipes.

The *MMC* changed JC's life in many ways. First of all, JC learned straight off how much sacrifice is needed for a show business career. He and his dad had to move down to Orlando, Florida, for six months out of every year while the show taped at the Disney-MGM Studios. As a child performer, he not only had to learn his songs, choreography, and acting lines, he was required to go to school on the set, too.

But JC says that he wouldn't trade the years he spent on *MMC* for anything!

"The friends I made on that show are lifetime friends," he says.

In fact, he sees one of those friends just about every day now. He's a kid that joined the cast of *MMC* two years after JC did. Maybe you've heard of him. His name is Justin Timberlake.

3
the making of 'N Sync

The Mickey Mouse Club shut its doors in 1993. After four seasons of acting, singing, and dancing with the other Mouseketeers, JC was now at a crossroads. He had considerable experience with both acting and music. Now it was time for him to decide which of those two talents he wanted to pursue.

JC finally came to an important decision. Music was where his heart was. So he picked up and moved to Los Angeles, one of the biggest music cities in the world.

JC spent only a few months in L.A., studying composition and songwriting with pros on the West Coast. But eventually, he got homesick, and took a plane right back to Maryland for a little r&r and a few home-cooked meals from mom.

JC's career path next led him south to Nashville, Tennessee, the city country music fans call Music City. Down in Nashville, JC continued his songwriting pursuits and sang on demo tapes for songwriters who were interested in submitting their songs to big-name country artists.

It was in Nashville that JC bumped into Justin again. The two former Mousekecuties were now working with the same Tennessee vocal coach on separate solo projects.

While JC and Justin were busy in Music City, their mutual friend Joey Fatone was still back in Orlando, singing his heart out for guests at the Universal Studios Florida theme park. Joey and JC had been friends for more than three years. They met when Joey was dating a costar of JC's from the *MMC*. (Joey was also an extra in a crowd scene in a music sequence shot for the *MMC*.) Joey and Justin had also met in Florida while both were performing. (Boy, Orlando is a small world, huh?)

While JC and Justin were off in Nashville, Joey had become close friends with another Universal Studios performer, Chris Kirkpatrick. Chris's job was singing fifties doo-wop music outside a restaurant in the theme park. Chris confided to Joey that he wanted to get a singing group together. Joey said he knew two guys who just might be interested.

So there you have it—the real deal on who started 'N Sync. Because JC is the lead singer on so many of the group's songs, people just tend to believe that he was the one who originally got the group together. But that's not the truth. It was Chris who first spoke to Joey about getting some guys together who could sing and dance. Then Joey called Justin. And it was Justin who brought JC into the mix.

"Everybody knew each other in a round-about way. It was just a matter of the order that everyone called each other. But Chris was the one who came up with the idea for the group," JC confirms.

It doesn't really matter who called whom. What matters is, the group we now know as 'N Sync was already in its infant stages.

Justin and JC flew back to Orlando soon after talking with Chris and Joey. From then on, the four guys were all business. They worked at getting their harmonies straight and their moves smooth. They focused themselves on finding a manager who was willing to work just as hard to bring the guys to the top of the charts as they were.

"The first year we were together we were struggling to find management," JC explained to *Teen Beat* magazine. "Joey would get off work at nine o'clock and we would go into this warehouse and rehearse from nine to one—straight singing and dancing all night. Plus during the day, in between times, we'd be doing just vocal rehearsals . . . We knew what we wanted and we concentrated on it."

But no matter how hard they worked, the guys still felt something was missing from their sound. Despite the fact that JC, Chris,

Joey, and Justin all had tremendous vocal range, none of them could "go low"—sing bass.

Justin called his vocal coach in Memphis, Tennessee, and asked him to recommend a bass man. He suggested James "Lansten" Lance Bass (how appropriately is this guy named?!) for the job. Lance flew out to Orlando and instantly hit it off with the others. The final piece of the puzzle was now in place. All the group needed now was a name.

It was Justin's mom who came up with that. While fooling around with words made up with the letters in the guys' names, Mrs. Timberlake discovered that the last letters of the guys' names (or nicknames, actually) formed the words 'N Sync. Judging by the way the guys' voices worked together (in sync) to form harmonies, the name seemed perfectly fitting.

Finally, JC, Justin, Joey, Lance, and Chris felt that they were ready to put together a demo tape to shop around to potential management companies. JC asked a few of his camera crew pals from his *MMC* days to help shoot the group's video. They taped the video at Walt Disney World's Pleasure Island and then recorded a demo tape. The tape included a few original songs and a cover version of "We Can Work It Out" by the Beatles.

The guys sent copies of the audio and video tapes to managers all over the Orlando area and then sat back and waited for someone to give them a call.

One of the people who received the 'N Sync demo package was business manager Lou Pearlman. Lou liked what he heard and sent the package to famed manager Johnny Wright. Johnny had an incredible track record with guy groups. He had managed New Kids on the Block in the early 1990s. The New Kids were the biggest group of their time, and they cleared the way for newer guy groups like the megasuccessful Backstreet Boys, who, by no small coincidence, were also an Orlando singing group managed by Johnny.

What is it about the former swampland known as Orlando, Florida, that attracts so many talented singers? JC thinks he may know the answer.

"It's a very different gig down here because of all the theme parks," he explains, referring particularly to Walt Disney World, SeaWorld, and Universal Studios. "You've got lots of singing and dancing jobs, so there are plenty of opportunities for everybody."

Of course, not everyone who comes to Orlando with a dream has the talent or dedication it takes to become a star. But Johnny Wright is the kind of guy who can look at a crowd of hopeful kids and spot the ones who are going to go all the way. Johnny Wright knows success when he sees it, and Johnny had a good feeling about the rough tape and video that landed on his desk. He signed 'N Sync up right away.

At first, Johnny's top group, the Backstreet Boys, were reportedly less than pleased with their new competition. The Backstreet Boys were used to being top dog at Johnny's management company. Now suddenly there was another five-member guy group vying for their manager's attention.

"I won't say that we didn't go through that phase," Johnny told the *Orlando Sentinel* about the Backstreet Boys' initial concerns. "After all, for so long we were this team together, and they were the only ones. But there's no animosity [between the groups]. The more vocal groups there are, the better it is, because the more variety [the fans have], the more music they can have."

Johnny worked hard in those early days to make sure that all of his performers got along. At one point he even placed members of both 'N Sync and the Backstreet Boys on the same side in a charity basketball game, just to show "that this is a family for the future." He even went so far as to predict, "I wouldn't dismiss the possibility of 'N Sync and the Backstreet Boys making a record together."

We can't wait, Johnny!

But back then, it was the Backstreet Boys who were on top. 'N Sync was only in its beginning stages, and Johnny felt the place for the fabulous five to start was in Europe. So he signed the guys to a record deal with BMG Records, a company with headquarters in Munich, Germany.

As JC boarded the plane for Germany, he could feel the excitement flowing in his veins. This was it! 'N Sync was going to record an album, and that would finally show the world what they were made of. No doubt about it. This flight was the start of something really big!

4

the world gets in sync with 'N Sync!

Okay, so by now you're probably asking yourself, why Germany? Why not just stay right here in the U.S. and shoot for the stars?

Well remember, this was 1996. It was a time when almost no one in the U.S. had heard of Hanson, the Spice Girls, or the Backstreet Boys. People in the states were still heavily into the Seattle grunge sound of Nirvana and Pearl Jam.

But the Europeans had already moved on to a cheerier sound. In Europe, pop was king.

"We'd had a lot of offers [from record labels], but the best one, and the people who made us feel the most welcome, were from Munich. So, we took the offer and ran with it!" JC explains.

According to JC, the Germans were absolutely crazy about dance music.

"It's a really big deal there," he explains.

The guys weren't in Germany for very long before BMG shipped them off to Cheiron Studios in Stockholm, Sweden, to record the song that was destined to become their first worldwide hit—"I Want You Back."

"We had just signed our record contract a week earlier," JC recalls. "All of a sudden we were in Sweden meeting with three really famous songwriters."

The writers JC is referring to are Denniz Pop, Max Martin, and Kristian Lundin, first-rate pop songwriters who created stellar material for performers like Ace of Base and Robyn.

The boys were thrilled with their first professional recording.

"We thought it was something cool because we think our voices have more of an

R&B feel. But when you mix it with that dance beat . . . you get something really different," JC told *All-Stars* magazine in March 1998. "It's something you can really dance to."

The guys stayed in Stockholm for the next three months recording their debut CD. Their schedule was really tight—sometimes they had only a single day to record a song.

In 1997, when *'N Sync* was released in Europe, the boys crossed their fingers and hoped for the best. The album's success did not disappoint them. It shot to gold status across the continent, and even reached the number-one spot on the charts in Germany.

After touring (and conquering) Europe during most of 1997, Johnny Wright decided that the boys had gathered enough experience to take on what some say is the toughest music market in the world. Johnny brought 'N Sync back to the U.S.

Coming home was a shock to the guys. They were surprised to find that absolutely nothing had changed. You see, in Europe, 'N

Sync had become so popular with the fans that they had to travel with bodyguards. But here in their own country, nobody really knew who they were. In some ways, their lack of notoriety was a good thing. It gave the guys an instant dose of reality—and kept their egos in check.

But Americans were about to discover the group all of Europe had been raving about for nearly a year. To get the ball rolling, RCA records (an American record company owned by BMG) started sending out press releases announcing the American release of 'N Sync. Then they arranged for the guys to be interviewed by every major teen magazine in America. By the time the U.S. version of 'N Sync was released on March 24, 1998, the U.S. market was primed and ready for an 'N Sync invasion.

As soon as the album was released, the boys went into touring mode, performing at, among other places, the world's largest indoor shopping center, Mall of America in Minneapolis, Minnesota.

"I Want You Back" began to climb slowly up the U.S. charts, hitting the *Billboard* Hot 100 (where it would remain for six months!). But even with that success, 'N Sync didn't seem to be making their mark the way they had in Europe. The guys felt like they needed some kind of magic to help boost their careers. And once again it was Disney magic that did the trick.

The group had been chosen to perform on the Disney Channel's *In Concert* series. JC was very excited at the prospect of performing live at Walt Disney World. It would be the first time he had performed there since *MMC* had shut down production five years before. It was like a homecoming. A triumphant homecoming!

JC and the other guys got the total star treatment from the folks at Walt Disney World. That included putting their handprints in the cement outside the Chinese Theater at the Disney-MGM Studios, and being the guests of honor in a confetti-filled parade down the theme park's Hollywood Boulevard.

JC and the rest of 'N Sync knew they had a lot riding on the live concert and its subsequent broadcast. This would be their best chance yet to get a huge American crowd to see them perform. The *In Concert* series had already featured performances by LeAnn Rimes, Jonny Lang, and Brandy, giving the show a huge teen following— which was just the audience 'N Sync was courting. But while teens can be loyal fans, they can also be extremely harsh judges; if they don't like what they're watching, they'll grab the remote and change channels very quickly.

'N Sync didn't want there to be any channel surfing during their big show, so they made sure they pulled out all the stops, capturing the audience early on with their infectious energy and exciting costume changes. At one point, JC, Justin, and Joey all did flips—in sync of course! By the end of the night, the guys had the crowd at Walt Disney World singing along with them!

When 'N Sync walked off the stage for the night, the guys were ecstatic. It had been an awesome show. Everything had clicked—the music, the dancing, and the audience. They were hopeful that the magic would come through in the broadcast version of the concert. But it would be a while before they would know for sure how well the show would do on TV, because the concert would not be broadcast on the Disney Channel for two months.

When *'N Sync In Concert* finally aired, it was more of a success than JC and the boys could ever have imagined. In fact, it was the Disney Channel's highest-rated concert show to date. Viewers loved 'N Sync's performance so much that the Disney Channel reran the concert special six times in 1998 alone!

Sales of the *'N Sync* CD shot up dramatically after the *'N Sync In Concert* special aired. Executives at RCA gleefully acknowledged that the televised concert had exposed 'N Sync to a whole new audience, and obviously that audience had liked what it had seen and heard. *'N Sync* entered the *Billboard* top ten and stayed there for more than six months!

Finally, near the end of 1998, the guys were presented with every performer's dream award—a platinum record, proving that one million copies of the *'N Sync* CD had been sold in the United States.

There was no doubt about it! RCA and BMG knew they had a major hit group on their hands. So they did what any smart record label would do. They rushed the boys back into the studio to record a new album.

5

ho! ho! ho!

RCA let the guys know that there was no time to waste in getting 'N Sync's second CD into production. It was already August, and the album had to be in the stores by November. There was no room in the schedule for delays. This was a Christmas album. It couldn't hit the stores in January, could it?

So, at a time when everybody else was diving into swimming pools and cooling themselves with ice cream, JC and his buddies were in the studio, singing "O Holy Night."

Of all the 'N Sync guys, JC was the most enthusiastic about recording the new album. It didn't matter one bit to him what month it was. "I think I could be in a Christmas mood any time of the year!" he exclaims. "It's my favorite holiday."

JC came up with a plan to make sure his buddies joined him in the Christmas spirit department. "We all started wearing Santa hats for a while and lighting red and green candles in the studio. We even had blinking [Christmas] lights," he recalls, laughing.

JC and Justin wrote a special song for the new CD. They called it "Merry Christmas, Happy Holidays." JC and Justin weren't the only two group members excited by the upbeat holiday tune. In fact, all five 'N Sync dudes were so sure that the song would be a holiday classic that they decided to release it as the CD's first video and single. (Look for Gary Coleman from the old TV show *Diff'rent Strokes,* who makes a surprise cameo appearance in this ho-ho-holiday video extravaganza!)

To top things off, the Disney folks once again stepped in to help boost the sales of an 'N Sync CD. They decided to include the group's "Under My Tree" song on the soundtrack for its Jonathan Taylor Thomas movie *I'll Be Home for Christmas*. They also scheduled 'N Sync to perform as part of their Christmas celebration on the Disney Channel.

On November 10, 1998, 'N Sync's second CD, *Home for Christmas*, hit the stores. It was an immediate success, shooting straight to the *Billboard* Top Ten, where *'N Sync* was still sitting pretty after more than thirty weeks. Suddenly the boys had two top ten CDs at one time. That's something that rarely happens—even to established stars.

As the clock struck twelve on New Year's Eve 1998, 'N Sync was already in the midst of a full-blown U.S. tour which, by mid 1999, would take them to major cities throughout the U.S. and Canada. Suddenly

JC found himself the lead singer of the undisputed number-one group in America. He had come a long way from that shy little boy who would only sing and dance for his mirror!

6
he's on fire!!

You might think that JC is sweet as a puppy dog, graceful as a cat, or as tuneful as a songbird. But the truth is JC is a red-hot dragon—at least according to Chinese astrology.

The theory behind the Chinese zodiac is that your birth year affects your personality and the type of career you might pursue in the future. Each birth year in the Chinese zodiac is named for a particular animal. The people born under each sign take on some of the characteristics of their birth animal.

Just in case this all seems a little improbable to you, consider this. JC was born in 1976, which was the year of the dragon.

Dragons are considered the most attractive animals in the Chinese zodiac. Even the biggest doubters out there have to admit that when it comes to looks, JC has no peer. Like a fire-breathing dragon, JC's piercing blue eyes will melt a woman's heart.

JC is aware of how much attention is paid to his looks, so he takes some time each day to do a little primping before going out in public. Take the way he cares for his hair. "I like to try new styles," he told *BOP* magazine, "but right now I am in a mixed-up routine. I'm either using gel or hair wax. Wax is nice because then your hair still moves around a lot."

People born under the sign of the dragon are by nature very lucky. That is certainly true in JC's case. While there's no doubt that JC has worked hard to get where he is today, even he cannot deny that there was a certain amount of luck involved. After all, almost no one gets the first role they ever audition for. But JC's *Mickey Mouse Club* gig was the exception to that rule.

"It was my first audition, but I scored it," he has said. "I got pretty lucky."

He also says that luck and fate had a hand in bringing 'N Sync together.

"I met Joey and Justin through *MMC*, so I guess you could say that *MMC* is ultimately responsible for 'N Sync getting together," he says. "It just seems like fate that we all came together like we did!"

Part of what first attracted the *MMC* producers to JC was his natural charisma—something that dragons have in abundance. Dragons are almost always the center of attention, which explains why the producers of *MMC* were able to focus on JC in a crowd of thousands of kids.

Like most dragons, JC has the ability to communicate equally well with ten people or ten thousand people—just ask any girl who has seen 'N Sync in concert. She'll tell you that she's certain that JC was singing just to her!

But dragons are too smart to depend

solely on their looks and charisma. They are incredibly success-oriented and will work harder than anyone to reach the top of their profession. They're not afraid of spending long hours working toward their goal. That's why JC really appreciates the experience he got working on *MMC*. He says his work on *MMC* has made him the performer he is today.

"*[MMC]* helped to prepare me for what I'm doing now," he explains. "We filmed several shows every week, so I'm used to a heavy work schedule. Also, we produced an album and toured quite a bit, so I already know what life on the road is all about."

JC knows that the real secret to success is "dedication, persistence, and hard work." That's why he rarely complains when the group's rehearsals go into overtime so the guys can try a few new moves or a more intricate harmony. But beware if things run late because someone in the group didn't arrive on time. Like most dragons, JC hates delays, and he can get annoyed or irritable when faced with unnecessary holdups. But JC doesn't expect anything more from his pals than he does from himself. "I'm real strict on myself," he admits. "I always want to be fresh."

Dragons are world travelers, which is a very good characteristic for a pop star to have. Dragons are prone to adventurous streaks which take them to far-off places that others wouldn't even dream of going to.

JC's love of travel developed early on with those road trips he and his family took when JC was in elementary school. Traveling by car allows people to see the world around them close up—something you can't really get on a plane or a train. You get a chance to taste different foods, hear different accents, and see different terrains up close. JC has often said that those car trips helped broaden his perspective on the world.

But traveling isn't always perfect, and JC admits that no matter how wonderful the hotel, he always misses his own bed. JC claims that his favorite hobby is sleeping, so you can imagine how upsetting that must be. Maybe that's why he often takes one of the stuffed animals that fans throw onstage back to the hotel with him. He cuddles with it until he falls asleep.

Traveling can have other obstacles to overcome as well, as JC discovered when the group was scheduled to sing in South Africa. Although JC found the group's trip to South Africa one of the most fascinating experiences he has ever had, he almost didn't make it. You see, you need to take three shots before you can get to South Africa, and JC hates needles! "I was freaking out!" JC admits.

Finally, one week before the group was scheduled to leave for South Africa, JC's four group mates dragged him to the doctor's office. "The nurse came in and I thought it was shot time," he recalls. "She broke out this thing, and I didn't know what it was. I thought it was a shot, so I just yelled and ran out the door. The other guys started laughing so hard. They were like, 'Come back! It's just the ear thermometer!' I was so humiliated. But needles invading your body, I just don't like it!"

Still, needles and lumpy beds aside, for the most part JC lists traveling as one of the best things about his job. Like most dragons, he likes the opportunity to meet new people that traveling gives him. Dragons are definite people people. They love to hang out in cafes (or in JC's case, coffeehouses) and talk to perfect strangers. Sometimes those strangers are just average folks. But sometimes they can be celebrities. After all, first-class terminals in airports are often filled with the rich and famous. And while you're waiting for a plane, there's not much else to do besides chat. That's what happened when the 'N Sync guys met the Spice Girls in an airport in Germany. JC went over and struck up a conversation with the girls.

"We recognized them from the video,"

JC explains. "We recognized Sporty Spice's hair. They were still so new with it, like us. We told them, 'We're going to record a really cool song!'"

That kind of confidence is something dragons are famous for. In China the dragon is always the leader of the carnival. The other group members often think of JC as a type of informal leader. They depend on JC to make sure they're all rested and ready for a photo shoot, or to check that they've got their music when they need it.

Dragons are innately honest people. They simply cannot lie. And while that is a wonderful trait, it can also get dragons into trouble, because they automatically assume that others are always truthful as well. And when a dragon is finally forced to face a situation in which he's been duped, he can get pretty angry—sometimes holding a grudge for years.

JC has often exclaimed that "the one thing I can't stand is lying." So, should you and JC ever hook up, be sure to always be truthful. It's the only way your relationship will ever work.

Dragons are the kinds of people who work hard at relationships and their careers. They are determined and ambitious, and destined for greatness. You could say that dragons are 'n syncable!

7
roar! *JC is king of the jungle!*

JC's birthday on the eighth of August places him right smack in the middle of the Leo zodiac sign. Unlike the other astrological signs, which are ruled by planets or the moon, Leo lions are ruled by the sun, the center of the universe. That may explain why Leos always seem to find themselves at center stage, even if that wasn't where they originally intended to be. In JC's case, that's proved totally true. (Remember how he went to those *MMC* auditions to provide moral support for a buddy, and wound up with a role on a national TV show?) Although he says there's no real stand-out star in 'N Sync, JC is often the center of attention in the group's live shows and videos.

When you're singing lead, all eyes are on you.

The signs of the zodiac are attached to one of four elements—earth, wind, fire, or water. Leo is a fire sign, and let's face it, when JC sings, he sets your heart on fire. When JC turns on the heat, there's no escaping his charisma.

People born under fire signs tend to be passionate about many things. JC certainly fits that bill. His passion for music is boundless, and so is his passion for people. He'll spend hours signing autographs and talking to fans. His only reward is the joy he feels when he sees them smile.

Professionally, Leos are equally at home in large and small situations. But socially, they are much stronger when dealing one on one. Put a Leo in a massive social situation, and he may lose some of his cool. Being a guest at a large party often requires a talent for small talk, something Leos are terrible with. Small talk is boring to them. They

(Anthony Cutajar / London Features)

Joshua Scott Chasez

'N Sync at the 1998 Billboard Awards

JC

"You're Driving Me Crazy"

(Miranda Shen/Celebrity Photo)

(Miranda Shen/Celebrity Photo)

(Chuck Pulin/Star File)

(Anthony Cutajar/London Features)

(Anthony Cutajar/London Features)

become irritable when asked to muse endlessly about the weather. Leos prefer heavy conversations about the many issues that are near and dear to their hearts. JC has said many times that the girl he finally falls for will be someone he can talk to about anything.

Leos make loyal and true pals. They see friendship as one of the most important bonds in life. That's part of the reason JC is so happy to be a part of 'N Sync.

"We're best friends. That's something that no matter what anyone says about us, they can't take away from us," he says of the group. "It's a chemistry we have—a bond. It's a genuine thing, and I think that's why people enjoy being around us."

Maybe, but the fact that the guys are talented and totally hunky doesn't hurt either!

Leos are enthusiastic about just about everything, and because they are natural leaders, their enthusiasm is contagious. Remember that time JC managed to get all the 'N Sync guys psyched for Christmas—in August?!

Leos are big on heaping on the praise. They know that people need positive reinforcement. After all, no one needs an extra pat on the back more than a Leo. That may explain why JC had to win a few competitions before he realized that he really was talented enough to sing for an audience. His parents knew it all along.

Leo lions are great organizers, and JC is no different. His neatness is a direct result of that desire to have everything under control.

Like most Leos, JC is an animal lover. Growing up, his family always had pets. JC was very attached to them.

"I had a dog, Grits, but he died about six months ago," JC told *BOP* magazine in 1997. "We still have a cat named Belle, but we haven't gotten another dog since."

JC's real family may never have gotten a new dog, but his 'N Sync buddies have recently adopted a dog from an Orlando animal shelter. The dog has been traveling with 'N Sync on their tour bus, and JC in particular loves to take care of him, taking the dog for walks and petting his fur. Wow! Who would have thought that was possible—a feline in love with a canine!

But then again, that's not so weird. Think about it—you've fallen in love with the lionhearted king of the (music) jungle. And why not? You're only human!

8
the number-one son!

JC Chasez has always been a responsible kind of guy. As a kid, he always did his homework when he was told to, cleaned his room when he had to (to this day he admits he's a real "neat freak"), and made it home by dinnertime after playing a neighborhood game of touch football. But that's not surprising. It's just the kind of behavior you would expect from a firstborn child.

Many scientists believe that a big part of a person's personality is formed because of the order in which they were born in their families. JC certainly has a lot of the characteristics that scientists have identified in a firstborn child.

Eldest children are born into a world of

adults. The firstborn child often grows up thinking of himself as a sort of little grown-up, taking on a lot of adult responsibilities.

It should come as no surprise then that the other members of 'N Sync think of JC as "Big Daddy." (They've even given him that nickname.)

"JC is the daddy of the group," Chris explains. "He's the one who's always like, 'I don't think we should go to this party tonight. We have a photo shoot tomorrow. We should stay in and get some rest.' He really takes care of us. He babies us."

Which doesn't necessarily mean that the other guys listen to JC all the time. After all, he's not *really* their parent. He's just one of the guys. But if the other 'N Sync-ers don't take JC's advice, they know they'd better beware! He calls them on it, every time!

"Then, the next morning, he'll just look at you and go, 'So you stayed up late last night. You're not going to look really good today are you?'" Chris adds.

Hey! Maybe that explains why JC is always the best-looking guy in the 'N Sync publicity shots!

But seriously, JC wants everyone to know that he doesn't mean to boss his group mates around. He's just trying to look out for their best interests.

"I'm not bossy," he swears. "I'm just into order."

Firstborn children are extremely close to their parents. After all, for a lot of their formative years, they didn't have to share their mom and dad with anyone. JC is no exception. He's so close to his parents, it's almost as if he worships them. JC lists his dad as the person who has been the most influential in his life, "because he has always been there for me."

JC credits his dad with a lot of his personal and professional success. "I respect my dad because he respects other people. He takes the time to listen to my point of view. My dad has always been really cool. He always says, 'if you ever need anything, let me know.' He's a solid individual. He's steady in what he does, and yet he is always looking for more to do and he's always looking to do something positive."

It was his dad, JC says, who taught him the most important lesson in his life— "Treat others like you would want to be treated." JC took that lesson seriously. These days he is a huge celebrity advocate for homeless families and children.

"If you think you have problems, try living out on the streets for a while," he tells his fans.

JC's parents were extremely supportive of their son's career plans. It was JC's mother who encouraged him to sing and take part in talent shows. And when JC got his big break on *The Mickey Mouse Club,* his mom and dad decided that the best way to keep the family together was for JC and his dad to go down to Florida while the show was taping. JC's mom stayed up north with Heather and

Tyler. The family stayed close by phone, and frequent visits during JC's shooting schedule.

Firstborn children often feel responsible for their siblings, and JC is no exception. To this day he continues to buy little gifts for his brother and sister from the places he visits. And he says that his best times on the road are the times his younger brother accompanies him. But JC can't really look out for Tyler and Heather the way he could when they were all kids living under one roof.

So instead, JC looks out for his band mates, making sure that there are no hurt feelings from things that are written in the press. Take the time when certain newspapers began referring to JC as 'N Sync's lead singer. JC made it a point to modestly tell reporters, "Everybody's got their own role and is a leader in some respect."

There's a seriousness about firstborn children that is rarely seen in children who are born in the middle or are the babies of the family. JC himself uses the words "serious" and "focused" when asked to describe himself, and his group mates agree.

"JC is hardworking and dedicated, and a very serious sort of person," Chris says. "I don't mean he's not any fun, but he knows when it's time to play and when it's time to work. He's really dedicated to his career, and that's very admirable."

Like a lot of firstborns, JC has acted like a grown-up for most of his life, and everyone who knows him kids him about it!

"You see, JC matured too quickly," Joey joked to a British reporter. "He peaked at the age of fifteen and he's going downhill slowly. All he wants to do now is sleep!"

9
tasty tidbits!

Full name: Joshua Scott Chasez
Nicknames: JC, Mr. Casual, Big Daddy
Birthday: August 8, 1976
Hometown: Bowie, Maryland
Hair: Brown
Eyes: Blue
Height: 5 feet 10½ inches
Shoe size: 11
Pets: None
Pajamas: Calvin Klein flannels
Jewelry: A silver necklace he purchased at
the King Henry's Feast medieval dinner
theater in Florida
Mother: Karen
Father: Roy
Younger sister: Heather

Younger brother: Tyler
Favorite food: Chinese
Favorite author: Shakespeare
Favorite color: Black
Favorite animal: Dog
Favorite cartoon: *South Park*
Favorite actor: Harrison Ford
Favorite actress: Meg Ryan
Favorite movies: The first three *Star Wars* movies and all three *Indiana Jones* flicks
Favorite model: Naomi Campbell
Favorite musicians: Stevie Wonder, Seal, Sade, Brian McKnight, Sting, Billie Holiday
Favorite collectible: Hard Rock Cafe menus
Favorite ice cream flavors: Mint chocolate chip and cookie dough
Favorite toy: Yo-yo. He can do the "walk the dog" and "around the world" tricks.
Favorite childhood memory: Playing hide-and-seek in the laundry basket at home
Favorite sport: Football
Favorite football team: Washington Redskins
Favorite workout: In-line skating

Favorite place: His bed, because he loves to sleep

Favorite holiday: Christmas—although he really procrastinates about buying presents, and winds up getting them at the last minute

Favorite article of clothing: Leather jacket

Favorite thing about being in a musical group: The friendship

Favorite hangouts: Jazz clubs and coffeehouses

Little-known fact: JC talks in his sleep. He once had an entire conversation with his sister while he was fast asleep.

Worst quality: He's a neat freak.

If he could go back in time he would go back to: The 1920s, when "everything was changing and getting really cool!"

Craziest thing he's ever done: Jumped off a school building (don't try this one at home!)

Can't stand: Liars!!!

Another little-known fact: He sings in the shower.

First love: A girl named Francy who he met when they were both fifteen.

If he could choose a super power: He would be invisible or telepathic.

Worst fear: Needles

Tattoos: None—he's afraid of needles, remember?

Favorite Spice Girl: Mel B. (Scary Spice). JC says, "She's one cool chick."

Yet another little-known fact: He dances and makes faces at himself in the mirror.

Bad habit: He chews his fingernails.

JC's idea of a perfect day: A whole day of undisturbed sleep

Age JC was when he got (and gave) his first kiss: Six

10
are you the girl of his dreams?

JC has been single for a very, very long time. In fact, he says he's only been in love once—and that was back when he was in high school.

"I was fifteen and so was she. Her name was Francy. She was a beautiful girl inside and out," he reminisces. "But in the end it was only a teenage thing. We left each other because I had to move away. It was so sad."

But it has been almost eight years since JC's big breakup. And he is finally showing signs that he is ready to start a new, intense relationship. Recently, a girl proposed to Justin during an on-line chat. Justin told the girl that he wasn't ready to get married just yet. But JC butted in, telling the girl, "Hey! I'm single!"

Could you be the girl to rebuild JC's long-broken heart? Well, if you are outgoing and spontaneous, you may just be the one! JC admits that as a certified workaholic who is totally focused on his music, he really needs to be with someone who is a lot of fun. He wants to be with a girl who can come up with ideas for exciting, crazy outings, and drag him away from his music.

"I need somebody who brings a little fun out of me—somebody who can make me laugh," he says.

JC is a firm believer that a girlfriend should be exactly what the word says—a *friend,* first and foremost. In fact, many of the characteristics he looks for in a girlfriend are the same ones he admires in his group mates.

"I look for the same things [in a girlfriend] as I do in a friend, really," he explains. "First of all, honesty. Second of all, somebody who can make me laugh, 'cause I'm a pretty serious person, and understanding, because this gig has us traveling to a hundred different places!"

JC also likes a girl who is confident and not afraid to voice her opinions—even if they differ from her man's. "Confidence is definitely an appealing quality," JC says. "I like a girl who says what she means, and voices her opinions. I love it when a girl carries herself well, and she's proud of who she is and what she does. You can see that confidence all the way across the room, because believe it or not, it's pretty rare."

But don't confuse confidence with conceit! When it comes to being JC's lady, stuck-up girls need not apply!

"There's a fine line between confidence and conceit," JC points out. "Nobody should ever cross it."

JC is fully aware that his passion for his career could be a real stumbling block in a relationship. But music is his number-one priority right now. Although they have already had two albums in the top ten, 'N Sync is still in the development stage of their career. That means the guys have got to focus their energies on the group. So the girl of JC's dreams will have to be very understanding.

"The most important quality for me these days is probably patience. A girl would have to be very patient to put up with my work schedule," he admits.

Does all that mean that JC doesn't really care what the girl of his dreams looks like? Well, not exactly. But JC swears that he's not looking for a drop-dead gorgeous model type. The first thing he notices in a woman is her face—especially her eyes and her smile.

One great way to get JC's attention is to send him a card or a gift that really stands out in a crowd. It doesn't have to be big or expensive. (Let's face it, anything you can buy for JC, he can probably afford to buy for himself, right?) Rather, you should go the homemade route—maybe writing him a poem or a song, or stitching up a cute one-of-a-kind stuffed animal that he can take back to the hotel and cuddle up with at night. But whatever you do, be sure to include a note that lets JC know how to get in touch with you. He just may want to send you a personal note to thank you for your very special gift!

Okay, so let's say that after a concert, you wait by the stage door until JC wanders out. You confidently bat your eyes, smile, and hand him a copy of a love sonnet you've written in the style of Shakespeare, his favorite author. You and JC hit it off, and suddenly, 'N Sync's most bodacious babe is asking you out on a date. Just what can you expect from a night on the town with JC Chasez?

Well for starters, don't expect a box of chocolates and a big bouquet.

"I guess I am [a romantic] to a certain extent, but I'm not like over the top," JC claims. "I mean, I'm not really a flowers-and-candy guy. But the only reason I'm not like that is I don't think it's all that original. I would do it, but I'd feel funny about it."

And don't expect JC to pick you up in a chauffeur-driven, big black stretch limo with a phone and a bar in the back. Big money dates aren't really his style either. He's more likely to drive up to your door in his own Jeep. (And you'd better hope he keeps a lid on that lead foot of his! Recently he was driving at eighty miles per hour in a sixty-miles-per-hour zone—and he wound up with a seventy-dollar speeding ticket!)

"I'm not Mr. Romeo who takes girls on yacht cruises and flies them on airplanes to go here and there," JC warns. "I'm more the kind of guy who goes for the little things."

Which is just fine with JC's fans. Just looking into those big blue eyes for an evening would be enough of a thrill for them!

So, now you know you won't be jetted to Paris for the weekend, or taken on a sunset cruise around Manhattan island. But where would JC take you for your night out?

"If I'm really into a girl I'll take her on a romantic date, maybe to see a play," he suggests. "I've even been known to serenade a girl with a song written especially for her."

Is your heart melting yet?

Well, hold on, because your evening is about to get better.

After the play, the night will still be young, and unless JC has a concert or a photo shoot the next day, he may want drive over to a jazz club where you two can listen to JC's favorite kind of music. Or maybe he'll drive off in the direction of a nearby coffeehouse for some quiet conversation. And here's where things can get tricky. After all, JC is into some pretty heady things, like Shakespearean plays and jazz. So before your big night, you may want to brush up on your *Romeo and Juliet* and listen to a few jazz albums, just so you'll be able to get the conversation going.

But don't try to fake the conversation by talking only about the things you think JC will want to hear. JC is a pretty intuitive guy, and he's going to quickly figure out that

you are being phony. The best advice on
how to behave on a date with JC is: Just be
yourself. Remember, JC values honesty
above anything else. And he will want to
learn all about the things that interest you.
When JC talks to someone, it's like there's
no one else in the room. He always takes a
genuine interest in other people.

And that's why we love him soooo much!

11
you've got jc's number!

We'll bet you think JC is #1! Well you're wrong. JC is actually a 6. It's true! The letters in JC's name make him a 6—at least in numerological terms. In every other way, he's a perfect 10!

The science of numerology dates all the way back to ancient Babylon. According to numerologists, a person's personality falls into one of 9 basic types. And you can find out what personality type your favorite star (which would be JC, natch!) fits into by counting up the letters in his name.

How did we figure out that JC was a 6? We wrote out all of the letters in his full name (nicknames will not give you an accurate numerological reading), and then matched the letters to the chart on page 77.

1	2	3	4	5	6	7	8	9
A	B	C	D	E	F	G	H	I
J	K	L	M	N	O	P	Q	R
S	T	U	V	W	X	Y	Z	

JOSHUA SCOTT CHASEZ
161831 13622 381158

Then we added all of the numbers in JC's name together, and got a sum of 60.

But we weren't finished yet. We added the 6 and the 0 (in 60) to get the number 6. That makes JC a 6.

If you want to find out what your numerological reading is, and whether or not you and JC are made for each other, add up your own numbers. (Remember to keep adding the numbers together until you get a single digit, since the personality traits are limited to the numbers 1 through 9.) Then find your number on the list below.

Ones, according to numerology, are natural-born leaders who are extremely well organized, and love the spotlight. But sometimes they can also get a reputation for being selfish and ruthless, so they have to learn to give up the limelight once in a while, for the sake of the whole team. Ones get along well with twos and sixes.

Twos are quiet people. They're well liked for their fair-mindedness and their ability to understand both sides of a situation. Twos make good friends especially because they have amazing memories and love to talk over old times. But twos can also be supersensitive. Criticism makes them brood over hurt feelings. Twos make good matches for sevens, eights, and other twos.

Threes are dynamic, exciting people. Everyone just wants to be around them. Threes like feeling comfortable in any situation, and they know how to make others feel that way, too. But these charismatic types often insist on having things done their way. Threes can have sharp tongues which sting. Everyone thinks they know all there is to know about a three, but nobody really does. Threes get along especially well with fours and fives.

Fours take duty and responsibility very seriously. But no one can ever say that they are dull and boring. Fours can be witty and entertaining, as well as being incredibly loyal pals. But they need to watch the annoying habit they have of saying exactly what's on their minds. Fours get along very well with twos, threes, and eights, but they really go for fives and sixes (which isn't really in their best interest!).

Fives are restless souls. They like action, adventure, and plenty of excitement. Fives are often the life of the party. Five are not great money managers, however. They tend to let their salaries slip right through their hands. Fives get along well with threes, sevens, and twos.

Sixes like JC spend a lot of time worrying about other people's welfare. That comes through in JC's personality, whether he's making sure that no one's feelings are hurt by things written in the press, or expressing his concern for the health of his group mates if they spend too many nights partying. It's hard not to like a six because they are so kind, even tempered, and eager to help. JC certainly comes through on all those counts— think about the way he helps the homeless!

Sixes tend to be truthful, but they forget that not everyone is. Sixes can be a little too trusting. People think of sixes as easy marks and tend to take advantage of them. Sixes need to develop a little more backbone. If you're a six like JC, spend some time hanging out with other sixes, ones, eights, and nines.

Sevens are trendsetters who are always full of new and exciting ideas. They can also be deep thinkers who love to delve into a subject. But nobody sets higher standards for themselves than sevens! Hey sevens: Lighten up!

People think sevens are snobby, but they're not, they're just really shy. Sevens get along well with nines, fours, other sevens, and eights.

Eights generally do pretty well in school. Eights are known to be highly disciplined people with intense powers of concentration. When they go for the gold, eights grab it every time. Eights never forget a kindness, but they never forgive an injustice either. Twos, fours, sixes, sevens, and nines go well with eights.

Nines are true humanitarians. They are extremely sensitive to world causes and the ecological state of the planet. But that can cause them problems, because often the needs of their close friends and family can take a backseat to their concern for humanity's big picture. Nines are likely to use their money and their seemingly endless stamina to help the world. But when it comes to a nine's own feelings, she's extremely mercurial—up one minute and down the next! Fours, sevens, and eights make great matches for nines.

12
music to his ears

If 'N Sync comes to your town, and the guys happen to have a night off, where do you think you might go to bump into JC? Well, the first place you might try is your local jazz club. JC's well known for his love of jazz music, so much so that the other guys in 'N Sync call him Mr. Jazz. When he's on the tour bus JC is usually listening to R&B and jazz on his Walkman, while his fellow band mates are listening to pop, rock, country, and rap. And that's really cool, because it is the group members' diverse interests in music that gives 'N Sync its unique sound.

If you want to get inside JC's head you really need to understand the music that is near and dear to his heart. So, to keep you

'N Sync with JC's musical tastes, we're about to give you a crash course in JC's favorite music. We've rounded up the 411 on all of his favorite artists and even recommended some classic albums by each of these singing sensations. That way, even if you don't meet up with JC, you can take comfort in the fact that there's always the chance he and you are listening to the exact same cut on the exact same CD at the exact same time. And how cool is that?!

Brian McKnight

It's hard to describe Brian McKnight. He's not just a singer. He's a songwriter, arranger, and producer, too. In fact, this guy is all talent, from his head to his toes.

Brian has been a musician ever since he could talk. He sang gospel in church as a child, and as a teenager discovered the brilliance of jazz music. (Is it any wonder he's one of JC "The Jazzman" Chasez's favorite musicians?!) Like JC, Brian has also been heavily influenced by the music of Stevie Wonder.

Over the years Brian has not only recorded his own albums, he has written and produced songs for famous R&B artists like Quincy Jones, Vanessa Williams, Take 6, and Boyz II Men. He's also recorded music with Mase and Sean "Puffy" Combs.

It's difficult to pinpoint Brian's unique sound, because his recordings range from gospel, to hip-hop, to reggae, to R&B. In fact, the only thing Brian's many contributions to the music biz have in common is that they are all top quality!

To hear the full range of Brian's talents, take a listen to *Brian McKnight, I Remember You,* and *Anytime.*

Stevie Wonder

If you want to know how it feels to be a music icon, Stevie Wonder would be the man to ask. Talk about staying power! It's been almost forty years since ten-year-old "Little" Stevie Wonder first wowed the A&R guys at Motown records with his brash singing style and keyboard finesse. Today, Stevie is still going strong, most recently recording with other, younger Motown artists like 98 Degrees.

Although Stevie has been blind since birth, he's never felt his lack of sight was a handicap. As a child he rode bikes and played games like all the other kids in his neighborhood. He also took piano lessons, and many people believe that his heightened awareness of sound has helped make him the musician he is today.

The list of Stevie's hits is so long it would practically take a whole book to list them all, but here are just a few: "You Are the Sunshine of My Life," "Living for the City," "Isn't She Lovely," "Sir Duke," and "I Just Called to Say I Love You."

Stevie Wonder is more than just a musician. He's a political activist, whose influence is so strong that he was instrumental in creating a national holiday celebrating the life of slain civil rights leader Dr. Martin Luther King. And he continues to espouse Dr. King's belief in nonviolence. Even though the trend in music has been toward anger and violence in the past few years, Stevie has never wavered, continuing to pour positive messages into his lyrics and his sound.

If you want a little positivity in your life (and you must, because *nobody's* message is more positive than 'N Sync's, right?), check out these Stevie Wonder CDs: *Talking Book, Innervisions,* and *Songs in the Key of Life.*

Billie Holiday

Nobody can say that JC doesn't appreciate the history of R&B. He's a true student of this brand of music, and no lesson in this combination of classic jazz and the blues would be complete without visiting the musical library of Lady Day (as Billie was called).

It's been more than forty years since Billie Holiday passed away, but she remains the undisputed queen of the blues. Billie did not have a powerful voice. Her voice was not particularly beautiful either. But she sang with an emotional intensity and pain that made the listener believe she was truly living the sad songs she sang. And chances are she really was. Billie had a very unstable life—her dad ran out on her family when she was a kid, and she never got over that feeling of abandonment.

As a grown-up, Billie continued to feel abandoned, this time by society. Billie lived during a time of racial segregation, and even when she was recording and performing with jazz greats like Benny Goodman and Artie Shaw, she could not stay in the same hotels or eat in the same restaurants as those white men did. She might have avoided her death in 1943 if she had been allowed into a nearby all-white hospital, instead of being transferred to a far-off facility that treated blacks.

If you're looking to hear some genuine blues at its best, place one of these platters on your CD player: *Billie Holiday Greatest Hits, Volume 1,* and *The Quintessential Billie Holiday, Volume 2.*

Seal

Some people might describe Seal's music as "Crazy," the title of his first huge hit single. But Seal says his music is about love. "No matter what position we occupy, whether we're rich or famous or sweeping the street, we all have the same need to love and be loved," Seal says of his sound. (Is it any wonder Seal speaks right to JC's sensitive, loving heart?!)

Seal is famous for taking a long time between albums, but that's because he puts so much care into every song he records. "I always want to give all I've got," he says.

Seal's incredible work ethic makes for

some amazing music. To see why JC thinks Seal is a "musical genius," take a listen to his debut album, *Seal*, and his emotional masterpiece, *Human Being*.

Sade

Sleek, classy, elegant—those are words that describe R&B star Sade physically *and* musically! (Coincidentally, those are the same words we've heard used to describe a certain dark-haired, blue-eyed, 'n sync-able star we know!) Sade has been a staple on the international jazz scene for more than ten years. As JC himself has said, "Sade has the most wonderful voice, and she's so beautiful. She can sing me to sleep anytime!"

Smooth jazz was not always Sade's style. Growing up in London's North End, she was more into funk, even heading up a jazz-funk collective called Pride, early in her career.

But it is as an R&B vocalist that Sade has made her mark, with tunes like "The Sweetest Taboo," "Jezebel," and "No Ordinary

Love." To get a sampling of this lovely lady's sound, pick up a copy of *The Best of Sade.*

Sting

At first glance, you might be a little surprised so see Sting's name on JC's list of top musicians. After all, unlike the other musicians that are near and dear to JC's heart, Sting did not get his professional start in R&B. In fact, he was a pop star in the 1980s with a group called the Police.

But if you think about it, 'N Sync is often considered a pop group themselves, although JC believes they lean more toward R&B in their sound. And like 'N Sync, the Police brought a lot of different musical styles into the pop world. They often combined reggae, soul, jazz, and even classical music with pop to create a unique sound.

After leaving the Police in the mid-1980s, Sting went out on his own and continued to experiment with all sorts of musical styles. He also went into acting, performing in more than a dozen movies, ranging from the Who's *Quadrophenia* to *The Adventures of Baron Munchausen*. (Remember, JC was required to do a lot of acting on *MMC*, which may also help explain his kinship with Sting.)

Like Stevie Wonder, Sting is an activist, lending his celebrity to causes like saving the rain forest and Amnesty International.

To get a full feel for Sting's multifaceted musical talent, try listening to *The Police Live!*, *The Dream of the Blue Turtles*, and *Mercury Falling*.

13
the jc trivia test!

Here's an easy question for you: Can you name JC's number-one fan? If you answered your own name, you're probably right. After all, now that you've read this whole book, you probably know more about JC than just about anyone!

Well, here's your chance to show off your JC IQ! We've stocked this Trivia Test with questions about all things JC. Some of the questions will seem pretty simple to a superfan like you. And many of the answers can be found somewhere within the pages of this book. But some of the questions are so difficult, even JC's mother may not know the answers!

When you have finished taking the test,

you can check your answers on pages 99–
102. Then take a look at the chart to see
how 'N Sync your score is with those of
other JC fans!

Okay, pick up your pencil. Be sure to
keep your eyes on your own paper. Here we
go!

1. True or False? JC's given name is Justin
   Scott.
2. Who is older, JC's sister Heather or his
   brother Tyler?
3. Name JC's parents.
4. True or False? JC sleeps with his childhood teddy bear every night.
5. What is JC's biggest fear?
6. JC says he sings like opera great Pava-
   rotti when he is where?
7. What does JC miss most when he is on
   tour?
8. What is JC's favorite personal posses-
   sion?
9. True or False? JC's favorite drink is
   water.

10. JC was in what grade when he got his first kiss?

11. True or False? JC is afraid of water.

12. In what country did JC meet the Spice Girls for the first time?

13. Is JC's belly button an innie or an outtie?

14. What does JC collect?

15. JC was on *MMC* during which seasons?

16. What were JC's two favorite childhood toys?

17. As a boy, where did JC love to hide when playing hide-and-seek?

18. True or False? JC considers himself lazy.

19. If JC could sing a duet with any woman, who would it be?

20. Which does JC prefer—live performances or singing in the studio?

21. When JC was in elementary school, what mode of transportation did his family use for vacations?

22. Who is JC's favorite author?

23. Why doesn't JC have many baby pictures?
24. What is JC's favorite type of food?
25. What is JC's favorite color?
26. True or False? JC auditioned for *The Mickey Mouse Club* on a dare.
27. Name the first song JC ever performed for an audience.
28. What is JC's favorite type of car?
29. Which other member of 'N Sync was on *MMC* with JC?
30. What is JC's favorite sports team?
31. True or False? JC has the 'N Sync logo tattooed on his chest.
32. True or False? As a kid, JC idolized Superman.
33. Who is JC's favorite Disney character?
34. Who sings lead with JC on "I Want You Back" and "Tearin' Up My Heart"?
35. JC didn't begin singing solos on *MMC* until he was on the show how many years?
36. What kind of athletic classes did JC take while working on *MMC*?

37. What does JC say is his favorite thing to do?
38. What grade was JC in when he went on his first date?
39. What is JC's zodiac sign?
40. JC performed on *MMC* with which member of the *Felicity* cast?
41. What famous pop group of the early 1990s did Johnny Wright bring to the top of the charts?
42. Which of these shows has 'N Sync not guested on?
    (A) *Live with Regis and Kathie Lee*
    (B) *The Tonight Show with Jay Leno*
    (C) *The Roseanne Show*
43. What sport did 'N Sync play during their competition on *MTV Rock n Jock Presents: The Game*?
44. *'N Sync In Concert* appeared on what cable channel?
45. When is JC's birthday?
46. Does 'N Sync travel mostly by bus or plane?
47. What type of animal did the 'N Sync

guys adopt from an Orlando animal shelter?

48. JC says his clothing style ranges from semiconservative to _____.

49. Which does JC prefer—straight plays or musicals?

50. If JC weren't a singer, what does he say he would be?

51. One of JC's prized possessions is a pin he got from a waitress in which London restaurant?

52. True or False? JC won his first talent show by singing "The Star-Spangled Banner."

53. What does JC say was his most embarrassing onstage moment?

54. Can JC ski?

55. What is JC's favorite cartoon show?

56. During the time the guys were recording *Home for Christmas*, what did they light in the studio?

57. Who cowrote "Merry Christmas, Happy Holidays" with JC?

58. Which family member does JC sometimes bring on tour with him?

59. True or False? As a child, JC sang with the Maryland Children's Choir.

60. True or False? JC plays piano and guitar.

61. Who first spotted the notice for the auditions for *MMC*?

62. Who turned down the chance to do a concert for the Disney Channel, opening the way for 'N Sync to do the show?

63. JC and Justin once worked with the same vocal coach in what southern city?

64. What does JC say that his friends want more than anything now that he is a star?

65. True or False? JC has the messiest hotel room of any of the 'N Sync guys.

Answers to the JC Trivia Test

1. False. It's Joshua Scott.
2. Heather

3. Karen and Roy
4. False. He sleeps with stuffed animals thrown to him by admiring fans.
5. Needles
6. In the shower
7. His own bed
8. His Walkman
9. True
10. First grade
11. False. In fact, he is a wonderful swimmer!
12. Germany
13. Innie
14. Hard Rock Cafe menus
15. 1991–1994
16. His LEGOS and a Raggedy Andy made for him by his grandmother.
17. In the laundry basket
18. False. In fact, he considers himself to be a workaholic.
19. Janet Jackson
20. Live performances
21. Cars

22. William Shakespeare
23. They were destroyed in a fire.
24. Chinese
25. Black
26. False
27. "Right Here Waiting For You"
28. Jeep
29. Justin
30. The Washington Redskins
31. False
32. False. It was Flash Gordon.
33. Mickey Mouse
34. Justin
35. Three
36. Gymnastics
37. Sleep
38. Seventh
39. Leo
40. Keri Russell
41. New Kids on the Block
42. C
43. Basketball
44. The Disney Channel

45. August 8
46. Bus. (They only go by plane if the gig is eight hundred or more miles away.)
47. A dog
48. Funky
49. Plays
50. A music engineer
51. The Hard Rock Cafe
52. False. He won as part of a dance act.
53. When his fly broke during a performance in Switzerland
54. Yes
55. *South Park*
56. Red and green candles
57. Justin
58. His brother Tyler
59. False. He felt it was too scary.
60. True
61. JC's mother
62. The Backstreet Boys
63. Nashville
64. Tickets to 'N Sync concerts
65. False. In fact he says he's a "neat freak."

How Do You Rate?

To find out how well you did on this tough test, first add up all of your correct answers. Then find your score below.

55–65 correct: You Got It! You and JC are totally 'N Sync!

34–54 correct: Wow! You really are crazy for JC.

20–33 correct: Not bad, but you need to spend a little more time reading up on JC.

10–19 correct: Hmmm. Seems you have a little homework to do. Pull out those teen mags and start reading up on JC and the rest of the guys in the group. Smile. It'll be a whole lot more fun than chemistry! (Unless you're talking about that special chemistry you hope to have with JC!)

0–9 correct: Yikes! What did you do—begin your reading at the end of the book? Sorry, but you've got to start from scratch! Hurry. Turn to page one and read this book from cover to cover. It's never too late to get into JC!

14
jc's as close as your keyboard

By now you must know that there are literally zillions of Internet websites dedicated to 'N Sync. (Okay, maybe not zillions, but you get the drift!) But did you know that there are also plenty of pages dedicated to your fave 'N Sync guy? (That would be JC of course!)

We've rounded up the addresses of some JC pages that no true fan should be without. Some have amazing pictures. Others have loads of fun facts. Some tell you all about JC's life, while others focus on his time on *MMC* or with 'N Sync. But they all have one thing in common—they are totally JC!

So take your time, and go through them all. But as always, when you are on the

Internet, play it smart. Feel free to e-mail other JC lovers. But never give out your real name, phone number, or address, and never, *ever* agree to an in-person meeting with anyone you meet through the Internet.

FYI: Websites tend to come and go. So by the time you check out some of these, they may have disappeared. But don't worry about that: new JC websites are popping up all the time!

The Unofficial JC Chasez Page
www. angelfire.com/mi/bigcheez

Meet JC Chasez
users.why.net/supergal/nsync/JC/

'N Sync's Big Daddy: The JC Chasez Page
members.tripod.com/~jcchasez/index.html

JC Chasez
www.gurlpages.com/nolabel/jonelle128/
jc.html

JC Chasez!
www.fortunecity.com/marina/finisterre/27/
sleepy/main.html

YMS JC Chasez
www.ymshomepage.com/today/bb/n_sync/
chasez.html

For the Boy Who Has Everything—JC Chasez
fly.to/luvin_JC

The Boy They Call JC
www.fortunecity.com/tinpan/kurtwood/
615/jcindex.html

JC Introduction Page
www.geocities.com/SunsetStrip/Plaza/
1987

MMC
www2.hawaii.edu/~lisakane/mmc.html

Justin and JC on MMC
www.geocities.com/SunsetStrip/
mezzanine/3856/mmc.htm

If you want to find out all the latest news about JC and the other guys in 'N Sync, the best place to go is their official website. You can leave an e-mail message for JC there, too. We promise that even if you don't get a personal answer, JC loves hearing from you. It's just that he gets *so* much mail that it would be physically impossible for him to answer it all.

"I write back and all of a sudden there are like a billion hits because I actually replied," he says of the huge amount of e-mail messages in his computer mailbox. But don't kid yourself. He's not complaining! "I think it's brilliant!" he exclaims.

'N Sync's official website is located at: www.nsync.com/index2.html

You can also find 'N Sync info at the group's RCA records site: www.bmg.com/rca/artists/nsync

Don't worry if you're not yet wired for the information superhighway. You can still get a card, poem, or message to JC that's for his eyes only. Write to him at one of the following addresses:

JC Chasez
'N Sync
PO Box 692109
Orlando, FL 32869-2109

JC Chasez
'N Sync
c/o The RCA Record Label
1540 Broadway
New York, NY 10036

JC Chasez
'N Sync
c/o RCA Records
6363 Sunset Blvd.
Hollywood, CA 90028

JC Chasez
'N Sync
c/o Trans Continental Entertainment
7380 Sand Lake Road
Suite 350
Orlando, FL 32189

15
the 'N Sync discography

CDs

'N Sync

European Debut CD

1. "Tearin' Up My Heart" 2. "You Got It" 3. "Sailing" 4. "Crazy For You" 5. "Riddle" 6. "For The Girl Who Has Everything" 7. "I Need Love" 8. "Giddy Up" 9. "Here We Go" 10. "Best Of My Life" 11. "More Than A Feeling" 12. "I Want You Back" 13. "Together Again" 14. "Forever Young"

'N Sync

U.S. Debut CD

1. "Tearin' Up My Heart" 2. "I Just Wanna Be With You" 3. "Here We Go" 4. "For The Girl Who Has Everything" 5. "God Must Have Spent A Little More Time On You" 6. "You Got It" 7. "I Need Love" 8. "I Want You Back" 9. "Everything I Own" 10. "I Drive Myself Crazy" 11. "Crazy For You" 12. "Sailing" 13. "Giddy Up"

Home for Christmas

U.S. Holiday Release

1. "Home For Christmas" 2. "Under My Tree" 3. "I Never Knew The Meaning Of Christmas" 4. "Merry Christmas, Happy Holidays" 5. "The Christmas Song" 6. "I Guess It's Christmas Time" 7. "All I Want Is You This Christmas" 8. "The First Noel" 9. "In Love On Christmas" 10. "It's Christ-

mas" 11. "O Holy Night" 12. "Love Is In Our Hearts On Christmas Day" 13. "The Only Gift" 14. "Kiss Me At Midnight"

Winter Album

European Holiday Release

1. "U Drive Me Crazy" 2. "God Must Have Spent A Little More Time On You" 3. "Thinking Of You" 4. "Everything I Own" 5. "I Just Wanna Be With You" 6. "Family Affair" 7. "Kiss Me At Midnight" 8. "Merry Christmas, Happy Holidays" 9. "All I Want Is You This Christmas" 10. "Under My Tree" 11. "Love Is In Our Hearts On Christmas Day" 12. "In Love On Christmas" 13. "The First Noel"

COMPILATIONS

Music from *Sabrina, the Teenage Witch*

"Giddy Up" is included on this soundtrack CD.

U.S. Singles

"I Want You Back," "Tearin' Up My Heart" (released only for radio), "God Must Have Spent A Little More Time On You," "Merry Christmas, Happy Holidays"

Disc Info

The U.S. *'N Sync* CD went platinum (one million copies sold) in August 1998. The Canadian and European versions of the debut CD went double platinum.

"I Want You Back," which debuted at number twenty-five, earned 'N Sync a gold record (five hundred thousand copies sold).

During the month December 1998, both *'N Sync* and *Home For Christmas* appeared on the *Billboard* Top Ten, a rarity for any group.

About the Author

Nancy Krulik is a freelance writer who has previously written biographies of pop music phenoms 98 Degrees, Taylor Hanson, Isaac Hanson, and New Kids on the Block. She is also the author of the best-selling *Leonardo DiCaprio: A Biography*, and the trivia books *Pop Quiz* and *Pop Quiz: Leonardo DiCaprio*. She lives in Manhattan with her husband, composer Daniel Burwasser, and their two children.

2070

Five

The members of Five, Britain's hot new boy band, met last year at a London talent search and things "just clicked." Since that fateful day, these lovable lads—Rich, Sean, Scott, Abs, and J—have carried out a full-scale British Invasion of the U.S. pop scene with their edgy blend of soul, hip-hop, rap, and some serious attitude, creating a unique sound that blows the competition away.

With the complete 411 on these bright British stars, this book will leave you "Satisfied"!

By Matt Netter

Available now!

Published by Pocket Books

POCKET BOOKS